★
ICONS

HAVANA STYLE

HAVANA

Exteriors Interiors

STYLE
Details

AUTHOR **Christiane Reiter**
EDITOR **Angelika Taschen**
PHOTOS **Gianni Basso/Vega MG**

TASCHEN

KÖLN LONDON LOS ANGELES MADRID PARIS TOKYO

Front cover:
In miniature: veteran car at the Casa La Guarida.
Back cover:
Chatting: telephone at the window in the Casa Emilio Rodriguez Valdes.

Couverture :
En miniature : voiture ancienne dans la Casa La Guarida.
Dos de couverture :
Bavardage : conversation téléphonique à la fenêtre de la Casa Emilio Rodriguez Valdes.

Umschlagvorderseite:
En miniature: Oldtimer in der Casa La Guarida.
Umschlagrückseite:
Plauderei: Telefonat am Fenster der Casa Emilio Rodriguez Valdes.

To stay informed about upcoming TASCHEN titles, please request our magazine
at www.taschen.com or write to TASCHEN, Hohenzollernring 53, D-50672 Cologne,
Germany, Fax: +49-221-254919. We will be happy to send you a free copy
of our magazine which is filled with information about all of our books.

© 2004 TASCHEN GmbH
Hohenzollernring 53, D-50672 Köln
www.taschen.com

Concept by Angelika Taschen, Berlin
Layout and general project management by Stephanie Bischoff, Cologne
Texts by Christiane Reiter, Berlin
Lithography by Horst Neuzner, Cologne
English translation by Pauline Cumbers, Frankfurt/Main
French translation by Thérèse Chatelain-Südkamp, Cologne

Printed in Italy
ISBN 3–8228–3465–3

CONTENTS SOMMAIRE INHALT

It is one of the world's most successful stage shows – running now for decades, evening after evening, at the same venue, but each day with different actors and dialogues: Sunset on the Malecón. The moment the promenade between the city and the Atlantic becomes immersed in a golden light, the kissing, dancing, drinking and celebrating starts along the quay wall. As if the life of the city were being presented in concentrated form – for a couple of hours at least, the Malecón becomes Havana's heart and soul. And like no other place in Cuba, Havana satisfies that craving. With streets, bars, squares in which life simply throbs – and with apartments which are not so much places of private retreat as public meeting points. In their homes in Havana people gather together their favourite people and their favourite things – whether they match one another or not. Chests of drawers from the colonial era stand next to sideboards from the 1950s,

THE JOY OF LIFE
Christiane Reiter

C'est l'un des spectacles les plus prisés du monde – tous les soirs, depuis des décennies, on le joue toujours au même endroit avec, à chaque fois, des acteurs et des dialogues différents : le coucher du soleil sur le Malecón. Lorsqu'une brume dorée commence à envelopper la promenade qui sépare la ville de l'Atlantique, les gens se mettent à s'embrasser, à danser, à boire et à faire la fête tout le long du mur du quai. On dirait un condensé de la vie citadine – pour quelques heures le Malecón est à la fois le cœur, le ventre et la tête de La Havane. La Havane exauce ce désir plus qu'aucun autre endroit à Cuba, avec ses rues, ses bars et ses places où la vie est intense – et avec ses maisons qui n'offrent aucune intimité, mais sont au contraire de véritables lieux de rencontre publics. Ici on rassemble tout ce qu'on aime, qu'il s'agisse de gens ou d'objets et qu'ils aillent ensemble ou non. Des commodes de l'époque coloniale côtoient des buffets des années cinquante, de vieux fauteuils à bascule sont rangés à côté de sièges en plastique

Es ist eines der erfolgreichsten Bühnenstücke der Welt – seit Jahrzehnten Abend für Abend am selben Ort aufgeführt, mit täglich wechselnden Darstellern und Dialogen: Sonnenuntergang am Malecón. Wenn die Uferpromenade zwischen Stadt und Atlantik in Goldnebel taucht, wird entlang der Kaimauer geküsst, getanzt, getrunken und gefeiert. Es ist wie ein Konzentrat des städtischen Lebens – für ein paar Stunden ist der Malecón Havannas Herz, Bauch und Kopf zugleich. Havanna stillt diese Sehnsucht wie kaum ein zweiter Ort auf Kuba. Mit Straßen, Bars und Plätzen, in und auf denen das Leben pulsiert – und mit Wohnungen, die keine privaten Rückzugsgebiete sind, sondern öffentliche Treffpunkte. In Havannas Häusern versammelt man seine Lieben und Lieblingsgegenstände – ganz egal, ob sie zusammenpassen oder nicht. Da stehen Kommoden aus der Kolonialzeit neben Sideboards aus den Fünfzigern, uralte Schaukelstühle warten neben wackligen Plastiksesseln, und verblasste Heiligenbilder

ancient rocking chairs loll beside wobbly plastic chairs, and faded pictures of saints hang alongside the face of Che Guevara. Fascinating in its morbidly vital mix of penury and superfluity, shabbiness and beauty, each room tells it own story. Preserving Havana's historical architecture is no easy task. Although art nouveau villas, art deco buildings or Miami-style palaces in districts like Vedado or Miramar still radiate great splendour and glamour, there is a shortage of funds for large areas of the city, above all, for the colonial La Habana Vieja. Admittedly, many architects have been harsh in their criticism of the old-new houses, fearing the birth of a Cuban Disneyland – but as long as the style of home furnishings shown in this book still exists, and as long as that stage show continues to run every evening on the Malecón, Havana will always be what it is: Cuba's most beautiful city – and not just at sunset.

branlants et des images de saints aux couleurs passées sont accrochées à côté de portraits du Che. Chaque pièce nous conte sa propre histoire et est un mélange à la fois morbide et bien vivant de pauvreté et d'abondance, de délabrement et de beauté. Conserver les bâtiments historiques de La Havane n'est pas une mince affaire. Si des villas Art nouveau, des édifices Art déco ou des palais style Miami de quartiers comme ceux de Vedado ou de Miramar révèlent encore leur splendeur, les moyens financiers sont limités pour d'autres zones et surtout pour le quartier colonial de La Habana Vieja. Il faut pourtant bien avouer aussi que certains architectes critiquent sévèrement ces vieilles maisons remises à neuf, redoutant la naissance d'un Disneyland cubain. Mais tant que vivra cette culture de l'habitat telle que nous la présente ce livre et tant que se déroulera le spectacle nocturne sur le Malecón, La Havane restera ce qu'elle est : la plus belle ville de Cuba et ce, pas seulement lorsque le soleil se couche.

hängen neben Che Guevaras Antlitz. Jedes Zimmer erzählt seine eigene Geschichte, fasziniert durch eine morbid-lebendige Mischung aus Bedürftigkeit und Überfluss, Schäbigkeit und Schönheit. Es ist nicht einfach, Havannas historische Bausubstanz zu erhalten. Zwar zeigen sich Jugendstilvillen, Art-déco-Bauten oder Paläste à la Miami in Vierteln wie Vedado oder Miramar noch immer in viel Glanz und Glamour, doch für weite Gebiete und vor allem das koloniale La Habana Vieja sind Gelder knapp. So mancher Architekt übt an den alten neuen Häusern scharfe Kritik und fürchtet die Geburt eines kubanischen Disneylands – doch so lange es noch eine Wohnkultur gibt, wie sie dieses Buch zeigt, und so lange das allabendliche Theaterstück am Malecón auf dem Spielplan steht, wird Havanna bleiben, was es ist: Kubas schönste Stadt – nicht nur zum Sonnenuntergang.

"…Now and then, a light from a house shone out, then disappeared again on the horizon beneath a sky which could not have accommodated even one more star…"

Reinaldo Arenas, in: *Viaje a La Havana*

«…Par moments la lumière d'une maison étincelait puis disparaissait à l'horizon, sous un ciel où aucune étoile supplémentaire n'aurait pu trouver de place… »

Reinaldo Arenas, dans: *Voyage à La Havane*

»…Ab und zu schimmerte das Licht eines Hauses auf und verschwand wieder am Horizont, unter einem Himmel, an dem nicht ein einziger weiterer Stern Platz gefunden hätte…«

Reinaldo Arenas, in: *Reise nach Havanna*

EXTERIORS

Extérieurs Außenwelten

10/11 Water as far as the eye can see: view of the Atlantic. *De l'eau jusqu'à l'horizon : vue de l'Atlantique.* Wasser bis zum Horizont: Blick auf den Atlantik.

12/13 Following his footsteps: in memory of Che Guevara. *Continuer à vivre selon son exemple : souvenir de Che Guevara.* Nach seinem Beispiel weiterleben: Erinnerung an Che Guevara.

14/15 Sacred space: fully refurbished church in Havana. *Lieux saints : église entièrement restaurée à La Havane.* Heilige Hallen: Rundum restaurierte Kirche in Havanna.

16/17 A volatile state: dilapidated colonial homes. *Au risque de s'effondrer : maisons coloniales tombant en ruine.* Wacklige Angelegenheit: Verfallende Kolonialhäuser.

18/19 All façade: shell of a building in the old city. *Rien que des murs : enveloppe d'un bâtiment de la vieille ville.* Nichts als Fassade: Entkerntes Gebäude in der Altstadt.

20/21 Blue walls and coloured glass: façade of a pretty town house. *Murs bleus et vitres colorées : façade d'une jolie maison de ville.* Blaue Mauern und buntes Glas: Fassade eines schönen Stadthauses.

22/23 Opposites: colonial and modern buildings side by side. *Les contraires : bâtiments modernes et coloniaux juxtaposés.* Gegensätze: Koloniale und moderne Bauten Wand an Wand.

24/25 Wedding-cake style: refurbished house in the old city of Havana. *Style de la sucrière : maison restaurée dans la vieille ville de La Havane.* Zuckerbäckerstil: Saniertes Haus in Havannas Altstadt.

26/27 After lunch: colourful metal chairs on a roof terrace. *Après la pause de midi : chaises en fer colorées sur le toit de la terrasse.* Nach der Mittagspause: Bunte Eisenstühle auf der Dachterrasse.

28/29 Terminus: an abandoned bus. *Terminus : un bus mis au rebut.* Endstation: Ausrangierter Bus.

30/31 All in green: a lovingly cared-for veteran car. *Toute verte : une voiture ancienne entretenue avec amour.* Ganz in Grün: Liebevoll gepflegter Oldtimer.

32/33 Old before new: a mix of styles and eras. *Ancien et nouveau : mélange de styles et d'époques.* Alt vor neu: Mix von Stilen und Epochen.

34/35 Soaring: Cuba's national flag and Che Guevara's face. *Grands comme une maison : le drapeau de Cuba et le visage de Che Guevara.* Haushoch: Kubas Nationalflagge und Che Guevaras Gesicht.

36/37 A load of vitamins: banana transporter. *Une bonne dose de vitamines: un chargement de bananes.* Eine Ladung voller Vitamine: Bananen-Transporter.

38/39 Brilliance: colourfully distempered houses. *Lumineuses : maisons bicolores.* Leuchtkraft: Zweifarbig getünchte Wohnhäuser.

40/41 The rural and the urban: colourful façade. *La campagne au beau milieu de la ville : façade colorée.* Ländliches mitten in der Stadt: Bunt bemalte Fassade.

42/43 Perfect symmetry: ceiling vaults as if made of folded paper. *Joliment symétriques : arcs du plafond ressemblant à du papier plié.* Schönste Symmetrie: Wie aus Papier gefaltete Deckenbögen.

44/45 Welcome home: entrance to Casa Fuster. *Bienvenue au nid : entrée de la Casa Fuster.* Willkommen im Nest: Eingang zur Casa Fuster.

46/47 Follow the colours: steps up to Casa Fuster. *Suivez les couleurs : cage d'escalier de la Casa Fuster.* Immer den Farben nach: Treppenaufgang zur Casa Fuster.

48/49 Swimming with a colourful view: the pool at Casa Fuster. *Se baigner avec vue sur des murs colorés : la piscine de la Casa Fuster.* Baden mit Blick auf bunte Wände: Pool der Casa Fuster.

50/51 All the colours of the rainbow: a façade like a work of art. *Toutes les couleurs de l'arc-en-ciel : une façade ressemblant à une œuvre d'art.* Alle Farben des Regenbogens: Eine Fassade wie ein Kunstwerk.

52/53 Standstill: imaginative immobile vehicle. *A l'arrêt : véhicule de fantaisie impossible à déplacer.* Stillstand: Unbewegliches Fantasie-Fahrzeug.

54/55 The day after: washing lines across the street. *Après le jour de grande lessive : cordes à linge tendues à travers la rue.* Nach dem Waschtag: Über die Straße gespannte Leinen.

56/57 Shabby splendour: stairway of the Casa La Guarida. *Une splendeur qui s'effrite : la cage d'escalier de la Casa La Guarida.* Abbröckelnder Glanz: Treppenhaus der Casa La Guarida.

"…The house is built of weathered boards. The doors and windows are low. In front of the altars blessed porcelain dishes shimmer in the humid heat, flanked by a Sony recorder and several Japanese ventilators…"

Joaquín Baquero, in: *Malecón*

«…La maison est composée de planches rongées par le temps. Portes et fenêtres sont basses. Des terrines de porcelaine brillent dans la chaleur moite devant les autels, encadrées par un magnétophone Sony et plusieurs ventilateurs japonais…»

Joaquín Baquero, dans: *Malécon*

»…Das Haus besteht aus verwitterten Brettern. Türen und Fenster sind niedrig. Geweihte Porzellanterrinen schimmern in der feuchten Hitze vor den Altären, flankiert von einem Sony-Recorder und mehreren japanischen Ventilatoren…«

Joaquín Baquero, in: *Malecón*

INTERIORS

Intérieurs Innenwelten

62/63 Filigree mosaics: colonial dining-room in the Casa Jair Mon Perez. *Mosaïque filigrane : salle à manger coloniale de la Casa Jair Mon Perez.* Filigrane Mosaike: Koloniales Esszimmer der Casa Jair Mon Perez.

64/65 A spot of red: fresh flowers on the chest of drawers. *Accents de rouge : fleurs sur la commode.* Rote Akzente: Frische Blumen auf der Kommode.

66/67 With ventilator and television: bedroom in the Casa Iluminada Hidalgo. *Avec ventilateur et téléviseur : la chambre de la Casa Iluminada Hidalgo.* Mit Ventilator und Fernseher: Schlafzimmer der Casa Iluminada Hidalgo.

68/69 A must in every Cuban home: a rocking chair. *Un « must » dans chaque maison cubaine : le fauteuil à bascule.* Ein „Muss" in jedem kubanischen Haus: Ein Schaukelstuhl.

70/71 Surrounded by saints: telephone at the Casa Iluminada Hidalgo. *Entouré de saints : le coin téléphone dans la Casa Iluminada Hidalgo.* Von Heiligen umgeben: Telefonplatz in der Casa Iluminada Hidalgo.

72/73 Triad: frame, clock and ventilator at the Casa Iluminada Hidalgo. *Trio : cadre, pendule et ventilateur dans la Casa Iluminada Hidalgo.* Dreiergespann: Rahmen, Uhr und Ventilator in der Casa Iluminada Hidalgo.

74/75 With the blessing of Jesus: kitchen sideboard in the Casa Miguel Alonso. *Avec la bénédiction de Jésus : desserte dans la Casa Miguel Alonso.* Mit dem Segen Jesu: Küchenanrichte in der Casa Miguel Alonso.

76/77 Hand-made: bed and side-table in the Casa Jair Mon Perez. *Fabriqués à la main : le lit et la table de chevet dans la Casa Jair Mon Perez.* Handgefertigt: Bett und Nachttisch in der Casa Jair Mon Perez.

78/79 Stucco from floor to ceiling: the salon of the Casa Miguel Alonso. *Stuc du sol au plafond : salon de la Casa Miguel Alonso.* Stuck vom Boden bis zur Decke: Salon der Casa Miguel Alonso.

80/81 A weakness for knick-knacks: the dining-room of the Casa Marietta Valdes. *Un faible pour les bibelots : dans la salle à manger de la Casa Marietta Valdes.* Ein Faible für Nippes: Im Esszimmer der Casa Marietta Valdes.

82/83 Substitute garage: bicycle shed at the Casa Miguel Alonso. *En guise de garage : coin à vélo de la Casa Miguel Alonso.* Statt Garage: Fahrradstellplatz in der Casa Miguel Alonso.

84/85 Sleeping with an open window: at the Casa Miguel Alonso. *Dormir la fenêtre ouverte : à la Casa Miguel Alonso.* Schlafen bei offenen Fenstern: In der Casa Miguel Alonso.

86/87 Maritime motifs: coloured windows of the Casa Angelina de Inastrilla. *Motifs marins : fenêtre colorée de la Casa Angelina de Inastrilla.* Motive des Meeres: Bunte Fenster in der Casa Angelina de Inastrilla.

88/89 Fading charm: at the Casa Angelina de Inastrilla. *Charme légèrement vieilli : à la Casa Angelina de Inastrilla.* Leicht verblasster Charme: In der Casa Angelina de Inastrilla.

90/91 Mirror-image: bedroom in the Casa Angelina de Inastrilla. *Reflet dans la glace : chambre de la Casa Angelina de Inastrilla.* Spiegelbildlich: Schlafzimmer der Casa Angelina de Inastrilla.

92/93 With patina: the kitchen of the Casa Angelina de Inastrilla. *Avec de la patine : dans la cuisine de la Casa Angelina de Inastrilla.* Mit Patina: In der Küche der Casa Angelina de Inastrilla.

94/95 Glowing red bed-cover: in the Casa Angelina de Inastrilla. *Dessus de lit rouge vif : dans la Casa Angelina de Inastrilla.* Leuchtend rote Bettdecke: In der Casa Angelina de Inastrilla.

96/97 Open view: work place in the Casa Iluminada Hidalgo. *Vue sans entraves : lieu de travail dans la Casa Iluminada Hidalgo.* Freie Sicht: Arbeitsplatz in der Casa Iluminada Hidalgo.

98/99 A rare luxury: icebox in the Casa Iluminada Hidalgo. *Un luxe rare : le congélateur de la Casa Iluminada Hidalgo.* Seltener Luxus: Eisschrank in der Casa Iluminada Hidalgo.

100/101 Attention to detail: richly embroidered cover and a pretty pillow. *L'amour du détail : couverture richement décorée et bel appuie-tête.* Liebe zum Detail: Reich verzierte Decke und schönes Kopfteil.

102/103 Two in one: wash and sewing room in the Casa Iluminada Hidalgo. *Deux en une : salle de bains et salle de couture dans la Casa Iluminada Hidalgo.* Zwei in einem: Wasch- und Nähzimmer in der Casa Iluminada Hidalgo.

104/105 Palatial: lilac covered chairs under a canopy of gathered fabric. *Des allures de palais : fauteuils lilas sous une étoffe drapée.* Palastartig: Lila bezogene Sessel unter einer gerafften Decke.

106/107 Swaying gently: a simple rocking chair in the Casa La Guarida. *Des courbes douces : sobriété d'un fauteuil à bascule dans la Casa La Guarida.* Sanft schwingend: Schlichter Schaukelstuhl in der Casa La Guarida.

108/109 Transformed: the former hall serves as a wash-room. *Métamorphosé : l'ancien hall sert de buanderie.* Verwandelt: Die ehemalige Halle dient als Wäscheraum.

110/111 Blue motto: perfectly matching furniture and accessories. *Le bleu est la devise : harmonie parfaite des meubles et des accessoires.* Blaues Motto: Perfekt abgestimmte Möbel und Accessoires.

112/113 Wall with blemishes: at the Casa Iluminada Hidalgo. *Mur avec quelques imperfections : la Casa Iluminada Hidalgo.* Wand mit Schönheitsfehlern: In der Casa Iluminada Hidalgo.

114/115 Patterned: imaginatively designed kitchen of the Casa Fuster. *Mélange de dessins : cuisine décorée avec imagination dans la Casa Fuster.* Mustermix: Fantasievoll gestaltete Küche der Casa Fuster.

116/117 Multi-coloured dining-room of the Casa Fuster. *Le pot de peinture a bien servi : salle à manger de la Casa Fuster.* In den Farbtopf gegriffen: Esszimmer der Casa Fuster.

118/119 Like a private museum: favourite pictures above the bed. *Tel un musée privé : les tableaux favoris au-dessus du lit.* Wie ein privates Museum: Lieblingsbilder über dem Bett.

"…Three small statues of saints watched from their window sill. Half concealed in the dark, they seemed to be smirking, as if they had just told one another a joke…"

Ivonne Lamazares, in: *Sugar Island*

«…Trois petites statues de saints regardaient depuis le rebord de sa fenêtre. A moitié dans l'ombre, elles semblaient sourire comme si elles s'étaient raconté une plaisanterie…»

Ivonne Lamazares, dans: Oublier Cuba

»…Von ihrem Fenstersims aus sahen drei kleine Heiligenstatuen zu. Halb im Dunkeln verborgen, schienen sie zu schmunzeln, als hätten sie sich einen Witz erzählt…«

Ivonne Lamazares, in: *Sugar Island*

DETAILS

Détails Details

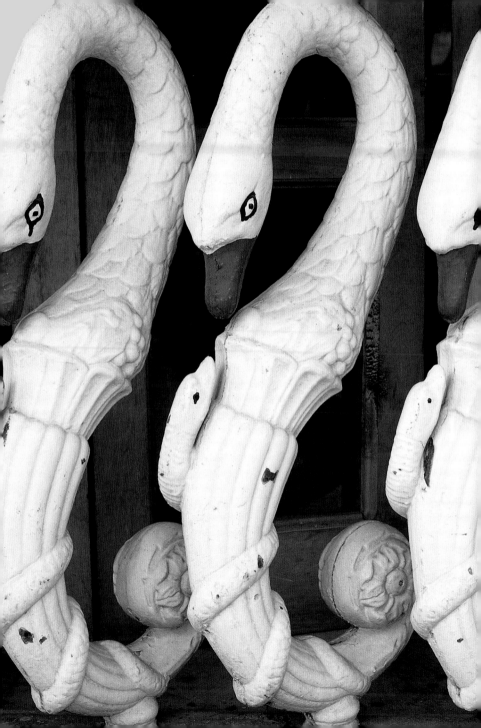

126 Quartet: four seats beneath a vaulted ceiling. *Quatuor : quatre sièges sous le plafond voûté.* Quartett: Vier Sitzplätze unter der gewölbten Decke.

128 Still going strong: a powder-blue veteran car. *Roule encore : voiture ancienne bleu ciel.* Immer noch fahrtüchtig: Himmelblauer Oldtimer.

129 Perfectly preserved: glass fanlights above the doors. *Parfaitement conservés : arcs en verre au-dessus des portes.* Perfekt erhalten: Gläserne Bögen über den Türen.

130 Apple green: accessories in the Casa Angelina de Inastrilla. *Vert pomme : accessoires dans la Casa Angelina de Inastrilla.* Apfelgrün: Accessoires in der Casa Angelina de Inastrilla.

132 Duet: two comfortable armchairs at the window. *Duo: deux fauteuils confortables près de la fenêtre.* Duo: Zwei gemütliche Sessel am Fenster.

133 Religious: picture of Jesus in the Casa Iluminada Hidalgo. *Religieux : image de Jésus dans la Casa Iluminada Hidalgo.* Religiös: Jesusbild in der Casa Iluminada Hidalgo.

134 Much in demand in the heat: a refrigerator. *Particulièrement prisé pendant la canicule : le réfrigérateur.* Bei Hitze heiß begehrt: Kühlschrank.

136 A shining example: sideboard in the Casa Angelina de Inastrilla. *Exemple lumineux : desserte dans la Casa Angelina de Inastrilla.* Leuchtendes Beispiel: Anrichte in der Casa Angelina de Inastrilla.

137 Comfortable: rocking chair in the Casa Angelina de Inastrilla. *Confortable : Fauteuil à bascule dans la Casa Angelina de Inastrilla.* Bequem: Schaukelstuhl in der Casa Angelina de Inastrilla.

138 In the corner: pedal scooter and tricycle. *Mis au coin : patinette et tricycle.* In die Ecke gestellt: Tretroller und Dreirad.

140 Bright red: fresh tomatoes in the Casa Miguel Alonso. *Rouge vif : tomates fraîches dans la Casa Miguel Alonso.* Knallrot: Frische Tomaten in der Casa Miguel Alonso.

141 Resounding: double-bass in the Casa Juan Carlos Cremata. *Un beau timbre : contrebasse dans la Casa Juan Carlos Cremata.* Klangkörper: Kontrabass in der Casa Juan Carlos Cremata.

142 Curving: stairs in the Casa La Guarida. *Dynamique : escalier dans la Casa La Guarida.* Schwungvoll: Treppe in der Casa La Guarida.

144 Seeing and being seen: television and photographs in the Casa Miguel Alonso. *Voir et être vu : téléviseur et photos dans la Casa Miguel Alonso.* Sehen und gesehen werden: Fernseher und Fotos in der Casa Miguel Alonso.

145 Former times: a radio in the Casa Miguel Alonso. *D'une époque révolue : radio dans la Casa Miguel Alonso.* Aus vergangenen Zeiten: Radio in der Casa Miguel Alonso.

146 A touch of Egypt: chairs in the Casa Iluminada Hidalgo. *Un air égyptien : chaises dans la Casa Iluminada Hidalgo.* Ägyptisch angehaucht: Stühle in der Casa Iluminada Hidalgo.

148 Stucco and sculpture: refurbished stairway in the Casa La Guarida. *Stuc et sculpture : cage d'escalier restaurée de la Casa La Guarida.* Stuck und Skulptur: Saniertes Treppenhaus der Casa La Guarida.

149 Refreshing: wash stand in the Casa Iluminada Hidalgo. *Rafraîchissant : coin pour la toilette dans la Casa Iluminada Hidalgo.* Erfrischend: Waschgelegenheit in der Casa Iluminada Hidalgo.

150 Modern technology: telephone-table in the Casa Angelina de Inastrilla. *Technique moderne : table de téléphone dans la Casa Angelina de Inastrilla.* Moderne Technik: Telefontischchen in der Casa Angelina de Inastrilla.

152 Well covered: artful lamp in the Casa Miguel Alonso. *Bel abat-jour: lampe artistique dans la Casa Miguel Alonso.* Gut beschirmt: Kunstvolle Lampe in der Casa Miguel Alonso.

153 Che Guevara is alive and well: in memory of Cuba's national hero. *Che Guevara vit : souvenir du héros national de Cuba.* Che Guevara lebt: Erinnerung an Kubas Nationalheld.

154 Chatting: telephone at the window in the Casa Emilio Rodriguez Valdes. *Bavardage : conversation téléphonique à la fenêtre de la Casa Emilio Rodriguez Valdes.* Plauderei: Telefonat am Fenster der Casa Emilio Rodriguez Valdes.

156 Ornate: metal archway. *Ajouré : arceau en fer forgé.* Verschnörkelt: Eiserner Torbogen.

157 Decorative: grille in front of the Casa Antonio Canet. *Richement décorée : grille devant la Casa Antonio Canet.* Reich verziert: Gitter vor der Casa Antonio Canet.

158 Three swans: dynamic sculptures. *Trois cygnes : sculptures aux formes élancées.* Drei Schwäne: Schwungvoll geformte Skulpturen.

160 White bars and coloured glass: an attractive window. *Barreaux blancs et vitrage de couleur : une fenêtre qui vaut le détour.* Weiße Sprossen und buntes Glas: Sehenswertes Fenster.

161 Heartening: vase in the Casa Samuel Weinster Trujillo. *Une affaire de cœur : vase dans la Casa Samuel Weinster Trujillo.* Herzensangelegenheit: Vase in der Casa Samuel Weinster Trujillo.

162 Pink: brilliantly painted cupboard in the Casa Miguel Alonso. *Rose bonbon : armoire peinte de couleur vive dans la Casa Miguel Alonso.* Pink: Leuchtend bemalter Schrank in der Casa Miguel Alonso.

164 A fine view: red balcony. *Une vue époustouflante : balcon en rouge.* Tierisch gute Sicht: Balkon in Rot.

165 Under pink arches: the centre of old Havana. *Sous des arcs de couleur rose : dans la vieille ville de La Havane.* Unter rosafarbenen Bögen: In Havannas Altstadt.

166 Fresh wind: ventilator in the Casa Iluminada Hidalgo. *Un vent frais : ventilateur dans la Casa Iluminada Hidalgo.* Frischer Wind: Ventilator in der Casa Iluminada Hidalgo.

168 Fragile: porcelain and glass in the Casa Jair Mon Perez. *Fragile : porcelaine et verrerie dans la Casa Jair Mon Perez.* Zerbrechlich: Porzellan und Glas in der Casa Jair Mon Perez.

169 Matching shades: rocking chair and mosaic in the Casa Jair Mon Perez. *Ton sur ton : fauteuil à bascule et mosaïque dans la Casa Jair Mon Perez.* Ton in Ton: Schaukelstuhl und Mosaik in der Casa Jair Mon Perez.

170 Personal: chest of drawers in the Casa Emilio Rodriguez Valdes. *Personnelle : commode dans la Casa Emilio Rodriguez Valdes.* Persönlich: Kommode in der Casa Emilio Rodriguez Valdes.

172 Cordial: window in the Casa Fuster. *Comme un cœur : fenêtre de la Casa Fuster.* Herzlich: Fenster der Casa Fuster.

173 Abstract art: at the Casa Fuster. *Art abstrait : dans la Casa Fuster.* Abstrakte Kunst: In der Casa Fuster.

174 Suitable frame: mirror in the Casa Angelina de Inastrilla. *Un cadre en harmonie : miroir dans la Casa Angelina de Inastrilla.* Passender Rahmen: Spiegel in der Casa Angelina de Inastrilla.

176 The twilight hour: at the piano in the Casa Emilio Rodriguez Valdes. *L'heure bleue : au piano de la Casa Emilio Rodriguez Valdes.* Blaue Stunde: Am Klavier der Casa Emilio Rodriguez Valdes.

177 A colourful bathroom: washsalon at the Casa Jair Mon Perez. *De la couleur dans la salle de bains : blanchisserie de la Casa Jair Mon Perez.* Mehr Farbe im Bad: Waschsalon der Casa Jair Mon Perez.

178 Sparkling: chandelier in the Casa Leonardo Cano Moreno. *Etincelant : lustre dans la Casa Leonardo Cano Moreno.* Funkelnd: Kronleuchter in der Casa Leonardo Cano Moreno.

180 Still-life: pianoforte, paintings and chandeliers. *Nature morte : pianoforte, tableau et lustre.* Stillleben: Pianoforte, Gemälde und Lüster.

181 Expressive: at the ballet studio. Très expressif: dans une école de danse. Ausdrucksstark: Im Ballettstudio.

182 Welcome: staircase of the Casa La Guarida. *Bienvenue : cage d'escalier de la Casa La Guarida.* Willkommen: Treppenhaus der Casa La Guarida.

184 Reading: in the salon at the Casa Juan Carlos Cremata. *Plaisir de lire : dans le salon de la Casa Juan Carlos Cremata.* Belesen: Im Salon der Casa Juan Carlos Cremata.

185 Shimmering red: curtains in the Casa Leonardo Cano Moreno. *Lueur rouge : rideaux dans la Casa Leonardo Cano Moreno.* Roter Schimmer: Vorhänge in der Casa Leonardo Cano Moreno.

186 Over-sized: balls of wool at the Casa Samuel Weinster Trujiillo. *Démesurées : pelotes dans la Casa Samuel Weinster Trujiiillo.* Überdimensional: Knäule in der Casa Samuel Weinster Trujiiillo.

The Hotel Book. Great Escapes Africa Shelley-Maree Cassidy / Ed. Angelika Taschen / Hardcover, 400 pp. / € 29.99 / $ 39.99 / £ 19.99 / ¥ 5.900

The Hotel Book. Great Escapes Asia Christiane Reiter / Ed. Angelika Taschen / Hardcover, 400 pp. / € 29.99 / $ 39.99 / £ 19.99 / ¥ 5.900

The Hotel Book. Great Escapes Europe Shelley-Maree Cassidy / Ed. Angelika Taschen / Hardcover, 400 pp. / € 29.99 / $ 39.99 / £ 19.99 / ¥ 5.900

"This is one for the coffee table, providing more than enough material for a good drool. Gorgeousness between the cover." —*Time Out*, London, on *Great Escapes Africa*

"Buy them all and add some pleasure to your life."

All-American Ads 40ˢ
Ed. Jim Heimann

All-American Ads 50ˢ
Ed. Jim Heimann

All-American Ads 60ˢ
Ed. Jim Heimann

Angels
Gilles Néret

Architecture Now!
Ed. Philip Jodidio

Art Now
Eds. Burkhard Riemschneider, Uta Grosenick

Berlin Style
Ed. Angelika Taschen

Bizarro Postcards
Ed. Jim Heimann

California, Here I Come
Ed. Jim Heimann

50ˢ Cars
Ed. Jim Heimann

Chairs
Charlotte & Peter Fiell

Design of the 20ᵗʰ Century
Charlotte & Peter Fiell

Design for the 21ˢᵗ Century
Charlotte & Peter Fiell

Devils
Gilles Néret

Digital Beauties
Ed. Julius Wiedemann

Robert Doisneau
Ed. Jean-Claude Gautrand

East German Design
Ralf Ulrich / Photos: Ernst Hedler

Eccentric Style
Ed. Angelika Taschen

Erotica 20ᵗʰ Century, Vol. I
From Rodin to Picasso
Gilles Néret

Erotica 20ᵗʰ Century, Vol. II
From Dalí to Crumb
Gilles Néret

Future Perfect
Ed. Jim Heimann

HR Giger
HR Giger

Havana Style
Ed. Angelika Taschen

Homo Art
Gilles Néret

Hot Rods
Ed. Coco Shinomiya

Hula
Ed. Jim Heimann

India Bazaar
Samantha Harrison,
Bari Kumar

Industrial Design
Charlotte & Peter Fiell

Japanese Beauties
Ed. Alex Gross

Kitchen Kitsch
Ed. Jim Heimann

Krazy Kids' Food
Eds. Steve Roden,
Dan Goodsell

Las Vegas
Ed. Jim Heimann

London Style
Ed. Angelika Taschen

Mexicana
Ed. Jim Heimann

Morocco Style
Ed. Angelika Taschen

Native Americans
Edward S. Curtis
Ed. Hans Christian Adam

New York Style
Ed. Angelika Taschen

Extra/Ordinary Objects, Vol. I
Ed. Colors Magazine

Extra/Ordinary Objects, Vol. II
Ed. Colors Magazine

15ᵗʰ Century Paintings
Rose-Marie & Rainer Hagen

16ᵗʰ Century Paintings
Rose-Marie & Rainer Hagen

Paris-Hollywood
Serge Jacques
Ed. Gilles Néret

Paris Style
Ed. Angelika Taschen

Penguin
Frans Lanting

Photo Icons, Vol. I
Hans-Michael Koetzle

Photo Icons, Vol. II
Hans-Michael Koetzle

20ᵗʰ Century Photography
Museum Ludwig Cologne

Pin-Ups
Ed. Burkhard Riemschneider

Giovanni Battista Piranesi
Luigi Ficacci

Provence Style
Ed. Angelika Taschen

Pussycats
Gilles Néret

Seaside Style
Ed. Angelika Taschen

Albertus Seba. Butterflies
Irmgard Müsch

Albertus Seba. Shells & Corals
Irmgard Müsch

See the World
Ed. Jim Heimann

Sneaker Book
Ed. Jim Heimann

Surfing
Ed. Jim Heimann

Sydney Style
Ed. Angelika Taschen

Tattoos
Ed. Henk Schiffmacher

Tiffany
Jacob Baal-Teshuva

Tuscany Style
Ed. Angelika Taschen

Women Artists
in the 20ᵗʰ and 21ˢᵗ Century
Ed. Uta Grosenick